NELSON

BY

PIETER VAN DER

snapping-turtle
guide

IN ASSOCIATION WITH THE NATIONAL MARITIME MUSEUM

DISCOVERY & EMPIRE

*W*hen Nelson was born in 1758, Britain was two years into the Seven Years' War with France. Latest in a long series with France or Spain, the main issue was who would be the world's leading colonial power and, by reaping the wealth of empire, dominate affairs in Europe. 1759, the 'Year of Victories', saw British victory in Canada and by 1763 part of India was also under Britain's control. The Royal Navy's role was crucial in gaining, developing and exploiting these possessions – by its own force, by that of the armies it transported and through the merchant fleets it protected. As Britain's empire grew, so did its navy and the need for improvement in all aspects of its work.

SAFER VOYAGING

After 1759 John Harrison's marine chronometer solved the greatest problem of ocean navigation – how to calculate accurate longitude east and west. This official copy of his H4 prototype, by Larcum Kendall, was used by Captain Cook on his last two Pacific voyages, between 1772 and 1779.

PRESS-GANGED!

The London press-gang rounding up men for the fleet in 1790. 'Pressing' was seen as unjust but a necessary evil in wartime. However, only seamen were liable to impressment. Others who were swept up and could prove they were not seamen were generally released.

CAT O'NINE TAILS

'The cat' symbolizes the harshness of naval life in Nelson's time. But it is often forgotten that life ashore could be much worse and that, to operate safely and effectively, sailing warships required unique skills and teamwork. Punishment played only a small part compared to mutual trust and good organisation.

NELSON'S KING

George III came to the throne in 1760, aged 22, and his 60-year reign saw Britain become the world's dominant seafaring power. Despite Nelson's part in this, his public and private behaviour meant the King rarely approved of him. Portrait by Sir William Beechey.

THE BATTLE OF QUIBERON BAY, 20 NOVEMBER 1759

The greatest naval victory of the Seven Years War, when Admiral Hawke routed the French fleet off southern Britanny, foiling plans for an invasion of Britain. This painting by Richard Paton shows the French *Thesée* sinking.

THE YOUNG NELSON

*H*oratio Nelson was born at Burnham Thorpe, Norfolk, on 29 September 1758, the third of five sons in a family of eight. His mother, whom he remembered with great affection, died when he was nine and he was educated at Norwich Grammar School and at North Walsham. Though small, he was from the first a spirited and determined daredevil.

NELSON AS A BOY

This miniature, by an unknown artist, is believed to show Nelson at the age of eight.

NELSON'S MOTHER

Catherine Suckling (1725-67) was the daughter of a Prebendary of Westminster and related to the influential Walpole family. A woman of strong character, this portrait shows her at the age of 18.

THE PARSONAGE HOUSE, BURNHAM THORPE

Nelson's birthplace was originally two big cottages with garden and glebe farm attached. Nelson also lived here with his wife while on half pay in the 1790s. The imagined group in the garden includes him as a boy with his parents. The house was demolished in 1802.

THE NELSON FAMILY BIBLE

Nelson had a very devout upbringing and remained deeply religious all his life. At the age of 17, while unwell at sea as a midshipman, he had a strange vision of 'a golden orb' which confirmed his trust in divine providence and determined him quite consciously to 'be a hero... and brave every danger'. Thereafter he was practically fearless for his own fate.

THE REVEREND EDMUND NELSON

Nelson's father (1722-1802) was a gentle, pious, strict and rather impractical man. His letters to his son are formal but affectionate and he developed a close relationship with Nelson's wife, Fanny. She persuaded Sir William Beechey to come and paint this portrait of him in 1800.

MIDSHIPMAN NELSON

Nelson joined the 64-gun *Raisonnable* at Chatham in March 1771, aged 12, following an offer from his uncle, Captain Suckling to start one of Edmund's sons on a naval career in his own ship. After early but inactive service, Suckling sent him to the West Indies in a merchantman to widen his experience. He then joined an Arctic expedition, after which he went to India in the frigate *Seahorse*, before he returned to pass his lieutenant's examination in London in 1777.

CAPTAIN THE HON. CONSTANTINE PHIPPS

Later Lord Mulgrave, he led Nelson's 1773 Arctic voyage in command of the *Racehorse* and formed a good opinion of the young midshipman. A portrait by Ozias Humphrey.

NELSON AND THE BEAR

One night Nelson and a companion left the *Carcass* without permission, to shoot a polar bear. Nelson's gun misfired and only a crack in the ice prevented the bear killing him before a cannon shot from the *Carcass* scared it away. To Captain Lutwidge's demand for an explanation, Nelson said he wanted the bear skin as a present for his father. From a painting by Richard Westall.

MIDSHIPMEN READING

A very rare image of 'young gentlemen' studying in the gunroom of the frigate *Pallas* in 1737, drawn by one of her lieutenants. But for the date and ship, Nelson could be one of these boys.

'UNCLE MAURICE'

Captain Maurice Suckling (1725-78) the brother of Nelson's mother, was a distinguished officer who rose to be Comptroller of the Navy. When told Nelson wanted to join the Navy he wrote: 'What has poor Horace done, who is so weak, that he...should be sent to rough it out at sea', but his early help was a great advantage to his nephew.

MIDSHIPMAN'S DIRK 1775

'Mids' carried these long dirks rather than swords. This one, 16in (40.5cm) overall, was sold by Banks of Plymouth Dock, now Devonport.

'THE LITTLE MIDSHIPMAN'

This carved wooden figure is the sign for an instrument seller's shop. It in fact shows a lieutenant in 1787 full-dress uniform, with his octant.

IN THE ARCTIC

In 1773 Nelson joined the *Carcass*, bomb vessel, one of two ships sent to seek a passage through the Arctic. Both were nearly trapped in the ice.

THE WEST INDIES

*N*elson's next years were spent largely in frigates, first in the *Lowestoffe* to the West Indies. He rose rapidly and in 1779 was appointed captain of the *Hinchinbroke*. In 1780 he returned home to recover from fever caught on a land operation in Central America. He then commanded the frigate *Albemarle* in the North Sea, to America and in the Caribbean. After a brief stay in France he returned to the West Indies in 1784 in the frigate *Boreas*.

CAPTAIN HORATIO NELSON, 1781

Painted for Captain Locker, by John Francis Rigaud, this was begun when Nelson was a lieutenant in 1779 and finished in 1781 when he was a captain.

CAPTAIN WILLIAM LOCKER
(1731–1800)

Nelson's captain in the *Lowestoffe*, who became his friend and mentor. Nelson later wrote: 'I have been your scholar...It is you who taught me to to board a Frenchman'.

NELSON AND COLLINGWOOD

Nelson (*left*) met Cuthbert Collingwood (*right*) when both were lieutenants in the West Indies. They remained lifelong friends, Collingwood being second-in-command at Trafalgar. These are pictures they did of each other in 1785.

NELSON BOARDING A PRIZE

When the *Lowestoffe* captured an American prize in November 1777 the sea was so rough the first lieutenant would not try boarding it. Nelson as second lieutenant did so. Richard Westall's picture shows him bidding farewell to Captain Locker as he leaves the *Lowestoffe*.

EVENTS OF NELSON'S LIFE

~1777 APRIL~
Passes for lieutenant. Appointed to *Lowestoffe* for West Indies

~1778~
France allies with American rebels

~JULY~
Joins *Bristol*, West Indies flagship of Admiral Peter Parker

~DECEMBER~
Promoted commander of *Badger*, brig

~1779 JUNE~
Promoted post-captain, in *Hinchinbroke*

~1780 JANUARY–APRIL~
Naval commander of San Juan River expedition. Appointed captain of *Janus* but too ill and returns sick to England

~1781 AUGUST~
Captain of *Albemarle* in North Sea

~1782 APRIL~
Sails for Canada

LOWESTOFFE,
32 GUNS, BUILT 1761

A fine original model of the frigate in which Nelson first served as a lieutenant under Captain Locker. Frigates had only a single deck of guns and were used as convoy escorts and scouts for the fleet. No admiral ever had enough of them.

SEEKING LOVE & FAVOUR

*I*n 1782 at New York, Nelson met Prince William Henry, third son of George III and a naval midshipman. He later served under Nelson in the West Indies as a junior captain when, to curry royal patronage, Nelson rashly supported him in a number of minor blunders. This, and Nelson's high-handed suppression of illegal trade between British merchants in the Caribbean and the newly independent United States, made him unpopular both there and with the Admiralty in England.

PRINCE WILLIAM HENRY

Shown here as a midshipman with Admiral Digby, the Prince became Duke of Clarence and, in 1830, the 'Sailor King' William IV. He and Nelson continued to correspond to Nelson's death, after which he wrote: 'I did not think it possible but for one of my dearest relations, to have felt what I have done, and what I still do, for poor Nelson'.

BOREAS OFF ST EUSTATIUS

Nelson commanded the 28-gun *Boreas* from 1784 to 1787. This drawing by Nicholas Pocock shows her off the Dutch West Indian island of St Eustatius, with a French frigate in the distance.

ADMIRAL LORD HOOD

Hood first commanded Nelson at New York in 1782 but cooled towards him after Nelson made himself unpopular for his zeal over the Navigation Acts. When war with France broke out in 1793 however, Hood, now a Lord of Admiralty, backed Nelson's appointment to the 64-gun *Agamemnon*.

FRANCES NELSON
(1761-1831)

'Fanny' Nisbet was the widow of a doctor, with a small son, and keeping house for her wealthy uncle on the island of Nevis when Nelson met her in 1784.

COLONIAL TRADE

A chart decoration, showing merchants and hogsheads of tobacco on a quay in Maryland. After 1783, direct trade between the now independent Americans and the British West Indian colonies was illegal. But it was also lucrative and tolerated, and Nelson's attempts to stop it made him enemies everywhere.

LIMERICK LACE OVERSKIRT OF FANNY'S WEDDING DRESS

In 1787, Nelson married Fanny on Nevis and, on return to England, they spent five years together at Burnham Thorpe until war broke out again in 1793, when their lives slowly became more separate. Fanny's anxiousness and inefficiency irritated Nelson, who needed practical arrangements at home and craved admiration.

REVOLUTIONARY WAR

*I*n 1788 Louis XVI summoned the French Parliament, which had not met since 1614. Within a year, the resulting drive for political reform triggered the French Revolution. Republican extremists seized power and in January 1793 a 'Reign of Terror' began with the execution of King Louis. In February, France declared war on Britain, Austria and Prussia.

RICHARD PARKER

In 1797 the British fleet mutinied for better conditions, first at Spithead (Portsmouth) and then at the Nore (Sheerness). Parker, shown here as a French Revolutionary, was among those hanged as leaders of the Nore mutiny.

VICTORY LEAVING THE CHANNEL

Seen flying Lord Hood's flag, outward bound with the fleet, including Nelson's *Agamemnon*, to support French Royalists at Toulon in 1793.

MADAME GUILLOTINE

The guillotine was introduced in Revolutionary France in 1792, as an egalitarian and humane means of execution. This 63lb (28.4kg) blade and sliding block is from one captured in the French West Indies in 1794.

EVENTS OF NELSON'S LIFE

~1793 JANUARY~
Louis XVI executed in Paris. French Revolutionary War starts

~JANUARY~
Appointed Captain of *Agamemnon*. Toulon and Mediterranean service. Meets Hamiltons at Naples

~1794 FEBRUARY~
Invasion of Corsica

~JULY~
Loses sight of right eye at Calvi

~1796 APRIL~
Appointed Commodore. Transfers to *Captain*

~DECEMBER~
In *La Minerve*; action with *Santa Sabina*

BATTLE OF THE GLORIOUS FIRST OF JUNE, 1794

Lord Howe's Channel Fleet's victory over the French Brest Squadron, 300 miles west of Ushant (Brittany), was the first major naval action of the war.

'SAILORS, THE REPUBLIC OR DEATH'

A flag from the boarding division of the French *L'Amérique*, one of the ships captured by Lord Howe at the Glorious First of June, 1794.

MARINS LA REPUBLIQUE OU LA MORT

'CONSEQUENCES OF A SUCCESSFUL FRENCH INVASION'

Detail from a print of 1810 by James Gillray, showing the French – by then no longer republicans but citizens of Napoleon's empire – setting up a guillotine in the old House of Lords, Westminster.

MORTELLA TOWER

The good anchorage in San Fiorenzo Bay, north Corsica, was guarded by an ancient watchtower on Mortella (myrtle) Point, with a heavy gun on top which fired red-hot shot. When attacked by Royal Naval ships in 1794 it put up such stiff resistance that it became the model for Britain's Martello Towers, built on the south coast from 1805.

NELSON'S WRITING

Nelson's regular and unexceptional right-hand script was quickly replaced after he lost that arm in 1797 by the spiky left-hand scrawl which is one of the most distinctive hand-writings of famous people.

NELSON'S SHIPS

An imaginary grouping at Spithead, showing his principal vessels from 1793. *Agamemnon*, 64 guns, is on the extreme left with *Vanguard*, 74, his Nile flagship broadside on and *Elephant*, 74, his temporary flagship at Copenhagen in front. In the distance is the *Captain*, 74, which he commanded as a commodore at Cape St Vincent and on the right *Victory*, 100 guns, his Trafalgar flagship. The picture is by Nicholas Pocock.

WAR IN THE
MEDITERRANEAN

*W*hile Hood's fleet besieged Toulon, Nelson in the *Agamemnon* patrolled the western Mediterranean, saw action against French frigates and in 1794 lost the sight of his right eye during the taking of Corsica. In July 1795 he distinguished himself in the capture of the French 80-gun *Ça Ira* and in 1796 he was appointed Commodore. By the end of the year, however, the British left the Mediterranean for strategic reasons.

CAPE ST. VINCENT & TENERIFE

*O*n 14 February 1797 the Spanish fleet attempted to sail from Cartagena to Cadiz. The British, now under Admiral Jervis, inflicted a severe defeat on them off Cape St. Vincent, with Nelson the hero of the hour. In July, Nelson (now Sir Horatio and a Rear-Admiral) led a risky attack on Spanish ships at Santa Cruz in the Canary Islands. It ended with retreat and the loss of his right arm.

'NELSON'S PATENT BRIDGE FOR BOARDING FIRST-RATES'

At Cape St. Vincent, Nelson in the 74-gun *Captain* almost single-handedly blocked the retreat of part of the Spanish force. This daring attack ended with his capture of the Spanish *San Nicolas*, 80 guns, and from her the 114-gun *San Josef*, as shown in the painting by Sir William Allan.

BELL OF THE *SAN JOSEF*

The *San Josef* was built of mahogany in Cuba, then a Spanish colony. After Nelson captured her she was taken into the Royal Navy.

NELSON BOARDS THE *SAN JOSEF*

With the *San Nicolas* entangled with the *San Josef*, Nelson ordered the charge to take her too. From a painting by George Jones.

NAVAL MEDAL

In 1794 the first modern naval medals were awarded to the admirals and senior captains at the Battle of the Glorious First of June. The same pattern was awarded for other actions, including Cape St. Vincent.

JOHN JERVIS, EARL OF ST. VINCENT (1735–1823)

Nelson's formidable superior commanded the Mediterranean and Channel Fleets and was First Lord of the Admiralty, 1801–05. He thought highly of Nelson as a fighter but came to disapprove of his political judgement and private life. By Sir William Beechey.

NELSON WOUNDED AT TENERIFE

While landing to seize Spanish ships in the harbour, Nelson's right arm was shattered above the elbow by a musket ball and was amputated that night. A painting by Richard Westall.

*I*n spring 1798, disturbing reports suggested that Napoleon was gathering forces at Toulon to attack Egypt and, beyond that, British interests in India. Nelson, now recovered from his wound, was sent to reconnoitre but missed the sailing of Napoleon's task-force in May, a few days before his flagship *Vanguard* was dismasted by a gale. With more ships from Jervis, he then spent the next two months searching the eastern Mediterranean for Napoleon's fleet. On the evening of 1 August 1798 he found and almost totally destroyed it in Aboukir Bay, near Alexandria, in the most crushing victory of his career.

NAPOLEONIC FURY

James Gillray's image of Napoleon swearing to extirpate the English after the Battle of the Nile, which trapped his army in Egypt until their defeat there in 1801.

THE BATTLE BEGINS

Nicholas Pocock's painting shows the French at anchor. Nelson's fleet is outflanking the head of their line, between the first ship and the Aboukir Fort, to attack on their unprepared side in what became largely a night action.

NILE FREEDOM BOX

This gold and enamel box was given to Nelson's flag-captain at the Nile, Edward Berry, with the Freedom of the City of London. It shows the battle with the French flagship *L'Orient* exploding.

LIGHTNING CONDUCTOR

From the mainmast of the French flagship, *L'Orient*, of Admiral Brueys. Nelson kept this as a souvenir of the Nile. The coffin in which he was buried was also made from the same mast.

TRIBUTES OF VICTORY

The musket and canteen were among the Sultan of Turkey's gifts to Nelson after the Nile. The silver cup by Paul Storr was presented to him by London's Turkey Merchants.

EVENTS OF NELSON'S LIFE

~1799 FEBRUARY~
Promoted Rear-Admiral of the Red

~JUNE~
Naples retaken. Savage Royalist reprisals. Created Duke of Brontë. Growing scandal of affair with Emma. Censured for delay in leaving Naples. Napoleon becomes First Consul of France

~1800~
Joins blockade of Malta

~JUNE-NOVEMBER~
To England overland with Hamiltons

CAPTAIN THOMAS FOLEY

Foley's *Goliath* led the outflanking manoeuvre which began the Battle of the Nile and was the key to its success. He was able to do this in shoal waters by having the most up-to-date local charts - ironically, French ones.

NELSON THE HERO

The most famous of Lemuel Abbott's portraits of him, painted after the Battle of the Nile from a sketch of 1797. It shows him wearing the diamond *chelengk* in his hat, awarded him by the Sultan of Turkey.

EMMA AND SIR WILLIAM

EMMA'S RING

Given to her by
Nelson, this is
gold with his
name spelt
out in
enamel
around it.

*A*fter the Nile,
Nelson made
a triumphant
return to Naples,
Britain's only Mediterranean
ally. He stayed with the British
ambassador, Sir William Hamilton
and his wife Emma, who engulfed
him in extravagant hero-worship.
Added to the effects of stress
and a head wound, the adulation
began to affect his judgement.
His relationship with Emma
rapidly became a passionate affair.

EMMA HAMILTON (C.1761–1815)

Emma was the daughter of a Cheshire blacksmith.
She had been a servant and artists' model before
becoming mistress of Sir William Hamilton at
Naples in 1786. They married in 1791. At the
time she met Nelson her manners and
appearance were likened to those of lively,
overweight barmaid.
This portrait by
Romney was
painted in 1785.

GIFTS TO EMMA

A bloodstone brooch of Nelson which she wore, a gold toothpick case which Nelson gave her at Christmas 1804 and a gold and enamel snuff box inscribed 'Dear Emma from NB'. The miniature, by John Dunn, shows Emma as she was when Nelson met her in the 1790s.

EVENTS OF NELSON'S LIFE

~1801 JANUARY~
Promoted Vice-Admiral of the Blue under Lord St. Vincent in Channel Fleet. Separates from wife. To Emma, a daughter, Horatia

~FEBRUARY~
In *St George*, joins fleet for Baltic under Admiral Hyde Parker

DRESS FLOUNCE

From a dress worn by Emma at a fete in Palermo, 1799. It has 'Nelson' and 'Brontë' (his Neapolitan ducal title) embroidered under swags of oak leaves.

SIR WILLIAM HAMILTON (1730-1803)

Hamilton was British envoy at Naples, 1764-1800. He pioneered the study of volcanoes and was a great collector of Classical vases. Much older than Emma, his second wife, he never acknowledged her true relationship with their mutual friend, Nelson.

'THE HERO OF THE NILE'

Nelson's vain but exhausted appearance after the Nile, weighed down with the sword and scarlet cloak given him by the Sultan of Turkey. By James Gillray.

NAPLES

aples - 'the Kingdom of the Two Sicilies'- comprised Sicily and most of Italy south of Rome, ruled over by the despotic and dissolute King Ferdinand IV. Late in 1798, when the French invaded Neapolitan territory, Nelson evacuated the royal family to Palermo. After a Royalist counter-attack, a truce with the French made by Ferdinand's war minister was cancelled by Nelson and the short-lived 'Vesuvian Republic' collapsed amid savage Royalist reprisals. These were condoned by Nelson who also had the turncoat head of the Neapolitan navy ruthlessly hanged at his own yardarm.

ROYAL REWARDS

Nelson was made Duke of Brontë in Sicily by King Ferdinand for his part in suppressing the Neapolitan revolt. This insignia of the Neapolitan Order of St. Ferdinand, and of Merit is the only one of his medals to survive. The rest were stolen from the Royal Naval College, Greenwich, in 1900.

REAR–ADMIRAL NELSON, 1799

This shows Nelson's exhausted appearance after the Nile and how he wore his hat to keep it clear of the forehead wound he received there. Painted at Naples by Leonardo Guzzardi.

FIDEI ET MERITO

ADMIRAL LORD KEITH

As new Mediterranean commander-in-chief he censured Nelson for his refusal to leave Naples when ordered, and strongly disapproved of his behaviour with the Hamiltons.

THE FLEET IN THE BAY OF NAPLES

An unusual view by an Italian artist, showing Nelson's squadron when it called at Naples while searching for Napoleon's fleet before the Battle of the Nile.

QUEEN MARIA-CAROLINA

Queen of Naples and sister of the executed French queen, Marie-Antoinette. She was talkative, pious, astute and practically ran Naples for her husband. Emma became her friend and confidante.

KING FERDINAND IV

He was mainly interested in hunting and women, and left government largely to his wife and half-English prime minister.

EVENTS OF NELSON'S LIFE

~1801 2 APRIL~
Battle of Copenhagen (in *Elephant*). Relieves Parker as Baltic commander in May. Created Viscount Nelson

~JULY~
Commands defence flotilla in South East England. Abortive attack on Boulogne invasion flotilla

~1802 MARCH~
Peace af Amiens signed

COPENHAGEN

After returning to England with the Hamiltons in 1800, Nelson was sent to the Baltic under Admiral Parker, to break a hostile alliance of Denmark, Russia, Prussia and Sweden. Neutralising the Danish fleet was the first task, achieved by Nelson with a detached force which Parker gave him. This bombarded the Danes anchored off Copenhagen until a truce was agreed. Nelson was rewarded with a viscountcy.

'I REALLY DO NOT SEE THE SIGNAL'

The hat Nelson wore at the Battle of Copenhagen and beneath which he raised his telescope to his blind eye, refusing to see Admiral Parker's signal to withdraw. The seal is the one with which he signed the offer of truce 'To the Brothers of Englishmen, the Danes'.

A DANISH TROPHY

This small brass gun was one of those taken at Copenhagen, though now on an English cast iron carriage. The opposing Danish force consisted of unrigged ships operating as floating batteries with two heavily armed offshore forts

'DIDO IN DESPAIR'

Gillray shows the now fat Lady Hamilton lamenting Nelson's departure for the Baltic, while on the other side of the bed Sir William Hamilton sleeps on. The title refers to the desertion of Dido, Queen of Carthage, by her lover Aeneas.

THE BATTLE OF COPENHAGEN

Nelson's line of 74-gun ships, anchored abreast of the Danes off Copenhagen on 2 April 1801.

THE MAD TSAR

Paul I of Russia, the mentally unstable Tsar, was a prime architect of the 'Armed Neutrality' of the northern powers against Britain. His murder nine days before the Battle of Copenhagen ensured its collapse.

EVENTS OF NELSON'S LIFE

~1802~
Settles at Merton with the Hamiltons

~1803 APRIL~
Sir William Hamilton dies

~MAY~
Napoleonic War starts (–1815)

COPENHAGEN 1801

MERTON

Gillray lampoons old Sir William Hamilton with emblems of his wife's infidelity in the guise of Classical antiquities.

*W*hen Nelson returned overland to England with the Hamiltons in 1800, Emma was already pregnant with his daughter Horatia, born in late January 1801. He abandoned his wife, despite her pleas for a reconciliation, and with Emma's help purchased Merton Place, a modest country house in what is now south-west London. When in England he, Emma and Sir William continued to live here together, to the scandal of respectable society. It was from Merton that he left for Trafalgar and his death in 1805.

HORATIA, AGED TEN

Nelson's daughter later married a clergyman and died aged 80, never knowing who her mother was, though she did realise Nelson was her father.

NILEUS

Among the various pets at Merton was a dog called Nileus, which in fact ran away not long after joining the household. This is his silver collar.

Lord Nelson NILEUS

26

HORATIA'S NECKLACE

A gift to her from Nelson. On another occasion she asked him for a dog and he sent her a gold one as part of a necklace decoration.

FROM NELSON'S HAND

One of his left-hand kid gloves with his name written in the cuff by Emma; his visiting card and the combined knife and fork he used after loss of his right arm.

EVENTS OF NELSON'S LIFE

~1803 JULY~
Joins *Victory* off Toulon as Commander-in-Chief in Mediterranean. Blockades French until early 1804

~1804 APRIL~
Promoted Vice-Admiral of the White

~MAY~
Napoleon proclaimed Emperor of France

~1805 MARCH-MAY~
French Toulon fleet and Spaniards from Cadiz escape to West Indies. Nelson pursues

~JUNE~
Combined Fleet resail for Europe, fight inconclusive action off Cape Finisterre with Calder's British squadron, 22 July, and enter Cadiz

CUP AND PLATE

A large quantity of Nelson's china survives. This plate and cup are from a Coalport service, the plate carrying his full coat of arms.

TRAFALGAR

n 1805 Napoleon ordered that Admiral Villeneuve's combined Franco-Spanish fleet make a diversionary expedition to the West Indies, before returning to cover an invasion of England. Nelson chased them there and back, to Cadiz, and the invasion plan was abandoned. The enemy fleet then sailed to support French forces in the Mediterranean and, on 21 October 1805, was defeated by Nelson off Cape Trafalgar.

Combined French & Spanish Fleet

British Fleet

'THE NELSON TOUCH'

Nelson's tactic was to attack in two lines, cutting off and overwhelming the enemy centre and rear before their vanguard could turn and assist.

TELESCOPE

Used at Trafalgar by John Pasco, *Victory's* signal lieutenant, who hoisted Nelson's famous signal; 'England expects that every man will do his duty'.

THE BATTLE OF TRAFALGAR

J.M.W. Turner's painting of 1824 is a Romantic interpretation of events rather than a record of them. It shows *Victory*, with the word 'duty' spelt out by the flags on her mainmast, and the captured French *Redoutable* sinking under her bows.

'KISS ME HARDY'

Shortly after 1.00pm Nelson was shot by a sniper and died about 4.30pm in *Victory's* cockpit. A.W. Devis's painting of his death shows Captain Hardy (standing) and the Rev. Dr Scott, Nelson's chaplain, rubbing his breast to relieve the pain. Walter Burke, the purser, supports the pillow and Nelson's valet, Guitan, looks at Dr Beatty who feels for the pulse.

NELSON'S PIGTAIL

'Pray let dear Lady Hamilton have my hair...', said the dying admiral. It was cut off after his death and is still tied in this queue at the back.

EVENTS OF NELSON'S LIFE

~1805 JULY~
Nelson reaches Gibraltar

~AUGUST~
Returns to England

~SEPTEMBER~
In *Victory* with fleet off Cadiz

~19 OCTOBER~
Combined Fleet leave Cadiz

~21 OCTOBER~
Battle of Trafalgar. Death of Nelson

~5 DECEMBER~
Victory, with Nelson's body, arrives home

FUNERAL

Nelson's body was returned to England in *Victory*, preserved in a cask of brandy. After lying in state in the Painted Hall of Greenwich Hospital, it was taken up-river on 8 January 1806 to the Admiralty in Whitehall. On the 9th, amid vast crowds and with the Prince of Wales leading the mourners, a huge procession bore it to burial in St Paul's Cathedral. Lady Hamilton's end was less glorious. Grief-stricken but ever-extravagant, she was imprisoned for debt in 1813. On release she retired to Calais, where, drinking heavily, she died in 1815.

IN MOURNING

John Salter, Nelson's jeweller, made 58 mourning rings for family and close friends attending the funeral. Some open to reveal a lock of his hair, though the example here is in a small brooch.

FUNERAL TICKET

Separate tickets were issued for the funeral procession and the service. This is the portrait painter John Hoppner's for the procession.

THE COFFIN

Nelson's body was enclosed in four coffins, the inner one made from *L'Orient*'s mainmast. This miniature was made on the *Victory* for her purser, Walter Burke.

SPANISH ENSIGN

This 50 x 32 ft (15.25 x 8.9m) ensign is from the Spanish *San Ildefonso*, captured at Trafalgar.

NELSON'S COLUMN

The column and statue were completed in Trafalgar Square, London in 1843. Their full height is 162ft 6in. (50m).

EVENTS OF NELSON'S LIFE

~1806 4-7 JANUARY~
Lies in state at Greenwich

~9 JANUARY~
Buried in St. Paul's Cathedral.

FROM THE FUNERAL CAR

The body was taken from the Admiralty to St Paul's on an elaborate carriage modelled on *Victory's* hull. This is its figurehead of Fame holding a laurel wreath.

NELSON'S FACE

A cast taken from a mould made at Vienna in 1800, as the basis for a bust, when Nelson was coming home overland with the Hamiltons.

DID YOU KNOW ?

Nelson's height – Nelson is often shown as small compared to others. Though slender, he was in fact about 5ft 6in (168cm), not short for his day.

'I have only one eye – I have a right to be blind sometimes. I really do not see the signal'. (At Copenhagen, 1801). Nelson is often said to have lost his right eye and is shown with a patch over it. In fact he only lost its useful *sight* and even this may have improved at the end of his life when he was more worried about the strain on his *left*. However, he did wear a shade over his right eye to reduce glare.

Nelson's Trafalgar signal – Nelson wanted to hoist 'England *confides* that every man will do his duty' but *Victory's* signal lieutenant, John Pasco, asked to use 'expects', which needed fewer flags. 'That will do', said Nelson, 'Make it directly'. His last signal was, 'Engage the enemy more closely'.

Nelson's last words – These were very carefully recorded. He did say 'Kiss me, Hardy' to his old friend and flag-captain. Hardy did so and then knelt again and repeated the gesture in farewell. He was not present when Nelson died, the admiral's last coherent words being 'Thank God I have done my duty'.

Nelson's body – Nelson's body was put in one of *Victory's* largest water casks, a 159-gallon leaguer, filled with brandy. This was topped up with 'spirits of wine' at Gibraltar before leaving for England. Dr Beatty later took out the fatal musket ball and, on his death in 1842, it was given to Queen Victoria.

Nelson's hero – The hero Nelson most admired was Major-General James Wolfe, who was killed aged 32 during his victorious attack on Quebec in 1759. Nelson asked Sir Benjamin West, who painted a famous picture of Wolfe's death, to record his own similarly should he be killed. West did so in 1806-07; it is now in Liverpool.

Admirals' ranks – Until 1864, admirals, vice-admirals and rear-admirals each had three levels of seniority according to 'squadronal colours' - red, white and blue. A captain, on promotion to 'flag-rank' became a Rear-Admiral of the Blue, then White, then Red before moving up to Vice-Admiral of the Blue. Nelson died as a Vice-Admiral of the White. The naval toast 'a bloody war or a sickly season' refers to the fact that, once a man had reached 'post' rank – (i.e. captain) promotion into 'dead mens' shoes' was automatic, even though continued active employment was not.

Ships of the line – Those considered large enough to lie in the line of battle and fight an opponent of similar size broadside to broadside. By Nelson's time the smallest was the 64-gun two-decker, such as the *Agamemnon,* and the largest the 100-gun three-decker, like *Victory*. Of all these the most useful all-rounder was the 74-gun ship, also a two-decker. Over half the fleet at Trafalgar was 74s.

ACKNOWLEDGEMENTS

Addax would like to thank: Liz Rowe, Graham Rich and Tracey Pennington for their assistance.
Photography by Tina Chambers and Peter Robinson, National Maritime Museum.

Nelson was published in association with the National Maritime Museum, Greenwich.
Copyright © 1995 Addax Retail Publishing Ltd
Text copyright © National Maritime Museum

We are grateful to the National Maritime Museum, Greenwich for permission to reproduce their copyright photographs for *Nelson,* with the exception of the following: page 31 Nelson's Column - C.O.I. Copies of the National Maritime Museum's photographs can be obtained from their Customer Services Section.

A CIP Catalogue for this book is available from the British Library. ISBN 1 86007 028 0